EMMANUEL JOSEPH

Edu-Play-tion, How Gaming and Spirituality Are Revolutionizing Education

Copyright © 2025 by Emmanuel Joseph

All rights reserved. No part of this publication may be reproduced, stored or transmitted in any form or by any means, electronic, mechanical, photocopying, recording, scanning, or otherwise without written permission from the publisher. It is illegal to copy this book, post it to a website, or distribute it by any other means without permission.

First edition

This book was professionally typeset on Reedsy.
Find out more at reedsy.com

Contents

1	Chapter 1: The Evolution of Education	1
2	Chapter 2: The Intersection of Play and Learning	3
3	Chapter 3: The Role of Technology in Gamified Learning	5
4	Chapter 4: Spirituality and Education	7
5	Chapter 5: The Science of Mindfulness in Schools	9
6	Chapter 6: The Benefits of Ethical Discussions	11
7	Chapter 7: Building Community Through Service Projects	13
8	Chapter 8: Creating Inclusive Learning Environments	15
9	Chapter 9: The Role of Teachers in Edu-Play-tion	17
10	Chapter 10: Measuring the Impact of Edu-Play-tion	19
11	Chapter 11: Challenges and Considerations	21
12	Chapter 12: The Future of Edu-Play-tion	23
13	Chapter 13: The Power of Storytelling in Education	25
14	Chapter 14: The Role of Creativity in Edu-Play-tion	27
15	Chapter 15: Global Perspectives on Edu-Play-tion	29

1

Chapter 1: The Evolution of Education

The history of education is a narrative of constant evolution. From the ancient methods of storytelling and apprenticeship to the modern use of technology, the way we impart knowledge has transformed significantly. In ancient civilizations, education was often informal and based on oral traditions. Knowledge was passed down through generations via storytelling and hands-on learning. This form of education allowed individuals to learn practical skills directly applicable to their daily lives.

As societies became more complex, so did the need for structured education. The establishment of formal schools and institutions marked a significant shift in the approach to learning. The ancient Greeks, for instance, emphasized the importance of a well-rounded education, incorporating philosophy, mathematics, and physical education. Similarly, the Islamic Golden Age saw the rise of universities and libraries, where scholars from different cultures shared knowledge and ideas.

The Industrial Revolution brought another major transformation to education. With the advent of factories and the need for a skilled workforce, education systems became more standardized. The focus shifted towards producing workers with specific skills and knowledge. This era also saw the rise of public education, making learning more accessible to the masses. However, this standardized approach often limited creativity and critical thinking, as the emphasis was on rote learning and memorization.

Today, we are witnessing another shift in education—one that embraces gaming and spirituality as key components. This change is not merely about integrating new tools but about rethinking our approach to learning itself. By understanding the roots of education, we can appreciate how these innovative elements are shaping its future. The integration of gaming and spirituality in education aims to create a more holistic learning experience that nurtures both the mind and the spirit.

2

Chapter 2: The Intersection of Play and Learning

P lay has always been a fundamental part of human development. From early childhood, games teach us problem-solving, social interaction, and creativity. In recent years, educators have begun to recognize the potential of integrating play into formal education. By gamifying lessons, teachers can engage students more deeply and make learning enjoyable. This chapter explores the science behind play-based learning and how it can be implemented in various educational settings.

The concept of gamification involves using game design elements in non-game contexts. In education, this means incorporating aspects like point scoring, competition, and rewards into the learning process. This approach taps into students' natural desire for play, making learning a fun and engaging experience. For example, teachers can create interactive quizzes, virtual treasure hunts, and educational video games to reinforce key concepts.

Research has shown that gamified learning can lead to increased motivation and retention of information. When students are actively engaged in the learning process, they are more likely to absorb and retain the material. Additionally, gamification promotes critical thinking and problem-solving skills, as students must strategize and make decisions to progress in the game. This active involvement in learning fosters a deeper understanding of the subject matter.

Implementing play-based learning requires careful planning and consideration. Educators must ensure that the games and activities are aligned with the learning objectives and curriculum standards. It's also important to create a balanced approach, combining traditional teaching methods with gamified elements. This way, students can benefit from the best of both worlds—structured learning and creative play. By embracing the intersection of play and learning, we can create a more dynamic and effective educational experience.

3

Chapter 3: The Role of Technology in Gamified Learning

Technology has revolutionized many aspects of our lives, and education is no exception. With the advent of digital platforms and interactive tools, gamified learning has become more accessible and effective. From educational apps to virtual reality experiences, technology provides endless opportunities to create immersive learning environments. This chapter delves into the different types of educational technology available and how they can be used to enhance traditional teaching methods.

One of the most significant advancements in educational technology is the development of educational apps. These apps are designed to make learning interactive and engaging. They cover a wide range of subjects, from mathematics and science to language arts and history. Students can practice skills, complete challenges, and earn rewards, all while learning at their own pace. Educational apps also provide instant feedback, allowing students to track their progress and identify areas for improvement.

Virtual reality (VR) and augmented reality (AR) are also making waves in the education sector. These technologies create immersive experiences that can transport students to different worlds and scenarios. For example, students can take virtual field trips to historical landmarks, explore the human body, or conduct scientific experiments in a virtual lab. VR and AR provide a hands-on learning experience that enhances understanding and retention of complex concepts.

Despite the many benefits of educational technology, there are also challenges to consider. Issues such as access to devices, digital literacy, and screen time need to be addressed to ensure equitable and effective implementation. Educators must also be mindful of the potential for distraction and ensure that technology is used as a tool to enhance, rather than replace, traditional teaching methods. By carefully integrating technology into the classroom, we can create a more engaging and effective learning experience for students.

4

Chapter 4: Spirituality and Education

Spirituality, often seen as separate from formal education, plays a crucial role in personal development. It involves understanding one's inner self, finding meaning in life, and developing a sense of connectedness with others. Incorporating spirituality into education can help students develop emotional intelligence, resilience, and a sense of purpose. This chapter examines various ways spirituality can be integrated into the curriculum.

One approach to incorporating spirituality in education is through mindfulness practices. Mindfulness involves paying attention to the present moment with an open and non-judgmental attitude. Research has shown that mindfulness can reduce stress, improve focus, and enhance emotional regulation. Schools can introduce mindfulness exercises, such as breathing techniques, meditation, and mindful listening, to help students cultivate a sense of calm and awareness.

Ethical discussions are another way to integrate spirituality into education. These discussions encourage students to think critically about moral dilemmas and develop their own values and principles. By engaging in these conversations, students learn to appreciate diverse perspectives, navigate complex issues, and make informed decisions. Educators can facilitate ethical discussions through case studies, debates, and reflective writing activities.

Community service projects offer students the opportunity to apply their learning in real-world contexts and make a positive impact on society. These projects promote teamwork, leadership, and a sense of civic duty. By participating in service activities, students gain a deeper understanding of their community and develop a sense of empathy and compassion. Schools can partner with local organizations to create meaningful service opportunities that align with the curriculum.

Incorporating spirituality into education requires a thoughtful and inclusive approach. Educators must respect the diverse beliefs and backgrounds of students and create a safe space for exploration and reflection. By fostering a sense of spirituality, we can help students develop into well-rounded individuals who are not only knowledgeable but also compassionate and resilient.

5

Chapter 5: The Science of Mindfulness in Schools

Mindfulness, a practice rooted in ancient traditions, has gained popularity in modern education. Research shows that mindfulness can improve students' focus, emotional regulation, and overall well-being. By teaching mindfulness techniques, schools can help students manage stress, enhance their concentration, and foster a positive learning environment.

The science behind mindfulness lies in its ability to activate the prefrontal cortex, the part of the brain responsible for decision-making and emotional regulation. Regular mindfulness practice has been shown to reduce the size of the amygdala, the brain's fear center, leading to decreased stress and anxiety. For students, this means better control over their emotions, improved attention span, and increased resilience to challenges.

Incorporating mindfulness into the classroom can be done through simple exercises such as deep breathing, guided meditation, and mindful movement. Teachers can start the day with a short mindfulness session to set a calm and focused tone for the day. Additionally, mindfulness can be integrated into various subjects, such as mindful reading in language arts or mindful observation in science.

By creating a culture of mindfulness, schools can provide students with valuable tools for managing their mental and emotional health. This holistic approach to education not only enhances academic performance but also supports the overall well-being of students and educators alike.

6

Chapter 6: The Benefits of Ethical Discussions

Ethical discussions encourage students to think critically about moral dilemmas and develop their own values and principles. By engaging in these conversations, students learn to appreciate diverse perspectives, navigate complex issues, and make informed decisions. This chapter highlights the importance of ethical discussions in fostering a sense of social responsibility and empathy.

Incorporating ethical discussions into the curriculum can be done through case studies, debates, and role-playing activities. For example, students can analyze historical events from different ethical viewpoints or debate contemporary issues such as climate change, human rights, and technology ethics. These activities promote critical thinking, empathy, and respectful dialogue.

Ethical discussions also provide an opportunity for students to reflect on their own beliefs and values. By examining their responses to ethical dilemmas, students gain a deeper understanding of their moral compass and develop the skills to navigate complex situations. This self-awareness is crucial for personal growth and responsible citizenship.

By fostering an environment where ethical discussions are encouraged, educators can help students develop a strong sense of integrity and social responsibility. This approach not only prepares students for academic success but also equips them with the moral foundation to contribute positively to society.

7

Chapter 7: Building Community Through Service Projects

Community service projects offer students the opportunity to apply their learning in real-world contexts and make a positive impact on society. These projects promote teamwork, leadership, and a sense of civic duty. By participating in service activities, students gain a deeper understanding of their community and develop a sense of empathy and compassion.

Service learning can be integrated into the curriculum in various ways. Schools can partner with local organizations to create meaningful service opportunities that align with academic goals. For example, students can participate in environmental clean-up projects, volunteer at shelters, or organize fundraisers for charitable causes. These experiences allow students to connect their classroom learning with real-world challenges.

Participating in service projects also helps students develop essential life skills such as communication, collaboration, and problem-solving. By working together to achieve a common goal, students learn the importance of teamwork and the value of diverse perspectives. Additionally, service projects provide opportunities for leadership development, as students take on roles and responsibilities within their teams.

Through community service, students gain a sense of purpose and fulfillment. They learn that their actions can make a difference and that they have the power to create positive change. This sense of agency fosters a lifelong commitment to civic engagement and social responsibility.

8

Chapter 8: Creating Inclusive Learning Environments

An inclusive learning environment is one that embraces diversity and ensures that all students feel valued and supported. This chapter explores the principles of inclusive education and how they can be applied in both gamified and spiritual learning contexts.

Creating an inclusive classroom begins with recognizing and celebrating the diverse backgrounds, abilities, and experiences of all students. Educators can promote inclusion by incorporating diverse perspectives into the curriculum and creating opportunities for students to share their own stories. For example, literature classes can include works by authors from different cultures, and history lessons can highlight the contributions of marginalized groups.

In addition to curriculum design, classroom practices play a crucial role in fostering inclusion. Teachers can create a welcoming environment by using inclusive language, providing varied learning materials, and adapting their teaching methods to meet the needs of all students. It's also important to establish clear expectations for respectful behavior and to address any incidents of discrimination or exclusion promptly.

Inclusive education also involves collaboration with families and communities. By building strong partnerships with parents and local organizations, schools can create a support network that enhances student learning and well-being. This collaborative approach ensures that all students have access to the resources and support they need to succeed.

By prioritizing inclusivity, educators can create a learning environment where every student feels valued, respected, and empowered to reach their full potential.

9

Chapter 9: The Role of Teachers in Edu-Play-tion

Teachers play a pivotal role in the successful implementation of gamified and spiritual education. This chapter examines the skills and qualities that educators need to effectively facilitate these innovative approaches.

To start, teachers must be open to change and willing to experiment with new teaching methods. This requires a growth mindset and a commitment to continuous learning. Professional development opportunities, such as workshops and training sessions, can help educators stay updated on the latest trends and best practices in gamified and spiritual education. By engaging in collaborative learning communities, teachers can share ideas, resources, and experiences with their peers.

Effective teachers in the realm of Edu-Play-tion also possess strong interpersonal skills. Building positive relationships with students is crucial for creating a supportive and engaging learning environment. Teachers must be able to connect with students on a personal level, understand their needs, and provide guidance and encouragement. This involves active listening, empathy, and effective communication.

Additionally, teachers must be adept at designing and facilitating interactive and experiential learning activities. This includes creating lesson plans that incorporate gamification elements and spiritual practices, as well as adapting these activities to meet the diverse needs of students. Flexibility and creativity are essential qualities for educators in this field.

By supporting teachers in their professional growth and providing the necessary resources, schools can create a culture of continuous improvement and innovation in education. This collaborative approach ensures that educators are well-equipped to inspire and empower their students through gamified and spiritual learning.

10

Chapter 10: Measuring the Impact of Edu-Play-tion

Assessing the effectiveness of gamified and spiritual education is crucial for understanding its impact and making informed decisions about its future. This chapter discusses various methods for evaluating the outcomes of these approaches, including qualitative and quantitative measures.

One common method for assessing gamified learning is through the use of performance data. This includes tracking students' progress, completion rates, and achievement levels in gamified activities. Data analytics tools can provide valuable insights into students' learning patterns and identify areas for improvement. Additionally, educators can use formative assessments, such as quizzes and interactive exercises, to gauge students' understanding and provide timely feedback.

For spiritual education, qualitative measures such as reflections, surveys, and interviews can help assess students' personal growth and development. These methods provide a deeper understanding of students' experiences, attitudes, and values. For example, students can reflect on their mindfulness practices, ethical discussions, and community service projects to articulate their learning outcomes.

Another important aspect of assessment is the evaluation of social and emotional learning (SEL). Tools such as SEL surveys and behavioral observations can help measure students' emotional regulation, empathy, and social skills. By incorporating these assessments into the overall evaluation process, educators can gain a holistic view of students' development.

Using data to inform instructional practices is essential for continuous improvement. By analyzing assessment results, educators can identify trends, strengths, and areas for growth. This data-driven approach ensures that teaching methods and curriculum design are aligned with the broader objectives of Edu-Play-tion.

11

Chapter 11: Challenges and Considerations

While the integration of gaming and spirituality in education offers many benefits, it also presents challenges. This chapter explores some of the potential obstacles and strategies for addressing them.

One common challenge is resistance to change. Educators, parents, and students may be skeptical about the effectiveness of gamified and spiritual education. To address this, it's important to provide clear evidence of the benefits and success stories of these approaches. Additionally, involving stakeholders in the planning and implementation process can help build trust and support.

Access to resources is another consideration. Implementing gamified learning requires access to technology and digital tools, which may not be available in all educational settings. Schools must ensure that they have the necessary infrastructure and support to effectively integrate these tools. This may involve seeking funding, grants, or partnerships with technology providers.

Concerns about screen time and digital distractions are also valid. While technology can enhance learning, it's important to strike a balance and ensure that students are not spending excessive time on screens. Educators can incorporate offline activities, such as mindfulness exercises and hands-on projects, to provide a well-rounded learning experience.

Incorporating spirituality into education may also raise concerns about respecting diverse beliefs and backgrounds. Educators must create an inclusive environment where all students feel comfortable exploring their inner selves. This requires sensitivity, open-mindedness, and a commitment to fostering a respectful and supportive atmosphere.

By acknowledging and addressing these challenges, educators can more effectively navigate the complexities of Edu-Play-tion and create a positive and impactful learning experience for students.

12

Chapter 12: The Future of Edu-Play-tion

The future of education is bright with the promise of gamified and spiritual learning. As we continue to explore and refine these approaches, we can create a more engaging, inclusive, and holistic educational experience for students.

Looking ahead, the integration of artificial intelligence (AI) and machine learning holds great potential for enhancing Edu-Play-tion. AI-powered tools can provide personalized learning experiences, adapt to individual students' needs, and offer real-time feedback. This technology can also help educators analyze data, identify trends, and make informed decisions to improve instructional practices.

Virtual and augmented reality will also play a significant role in the future of education. These immersive technologies can create dynamic and interactive learning environments, allowing students to explore new worlds and engage with complex concepts in a hands-on manner. As these technologies become more accessible, they will open up new possibilities for gamified and experiential learning.

In addition to technological advancements, the future of Edu-Play-tion will be shaped by a continued emphasis on social and emotional learning. Schools will prioritize the development of students' emotional intelligence, resilience, and empathy. By fostering a sense of purpose and connectedness, educators can help students navigate the challenges of the modern world and contribute positively to society.

Collaboration between educators, policymakers, and communities will be essential for realizing the full potential of Edu-Play-tion. By working together, we can create a supportive and innovative educational ecosystem that nurtures the growth and well-being of all students.

As we embrace innovation and stay committed to continuous improvement, we can revolutionize education for generations to come. The future of Edu-Play-tion is not just about adopting new tools but about reimagining the very essence of learning and personal development.

13

Chapter 13: The Power of Storytelling in Education

Storytelling has been a fundamental part of human culture since ancient times. It is a powerful tool for conveying knowledge, values, and experiences. In the context of education, storytelling can be used to engage students, enhance their understanding, and make learning more meaningful. This chapter explores the role of storytelling in gamified and spiritual education.

In gamified learning, storytelling can be used to create immersive and interactive experiences. By incorporating narratives into educational games, teachers can capture students' attention and motivate them to learn. For example, a math game might involve solving puzzles to help a character on a quest, while a history lesson could be framed as a time-traveling adventure. These narratives make learning fun and relatable, encouraging students to connect with the material on a deeper level.

Storytelling is also a powerful tool for teaching spirituality and ethical values. Through stories, students can explore complex moral dilemmas and reflect on their own beliefs and actions. Teachers can use stories from different cultures and traditions to foster empathy and appreciation for diverse perspectives. Additionally, storytelling can be a way for students to express their own experiences and connect with their peers on a personal level.

By incorporating storytelling into education, we can create a richer and more engaging learning experience that resonates with students and helps them develop a deeper understanding of themselves and the world around them.

14

Chapter 14: The Role of Creativity in Edu-Play-tion

Creativity is a vital skill for success in the 21st century. It involves the ability to think outside the box, generate new ideas, and solve problems in innovative ways. In the context of Edu-Play-tion, fostering creativity is essential for engaging students and helping them develop critical thinking skills. This chapter explores how gamified and spiritual education can nurture creativity in students.

Gamified learning environments provide numerous opportunities for creative expression. By designing their own games, creating digital art, or developing interactive stories, students can explore their creativity and apply their knowledge in unique ways. These activities encourage students to experiment, take risks, and learn from their mistakes. Additionally, games often require strategic thinking and problem-solving, which further enhances students' creative abilities.

Spiritual education also plays a crucial role in fostering creativity. Practices such as meditation, journaling, and reflective writing can help students connect with their inner selves and unlock their creative potential. By exploring their thoughts and emotions, students can gain new insights and develop a deeper understanding of their creative processes. Ethical discussions and community service projects also provide opportunities for students to think creatively about solving real-world problems.

By nurturing creativity through Edu-Play-tion, we can help students develop the skills they need to succeed in a rapidly changing world and inspire them to become innovative thinkers and problem solvers.

15

Chapter 15: Global Perspectives on Edu-Play-tion

Education is a universal endeavor, but the approaches to teaching and learning can vary significantly across cultures. This chapter explores how different countries and cultures are embracing gamified and spiritual education and the unique perspectives they bring to the concept of Edu-Play-tion.

In many Asian countries, for example, there is a strong emphasis on holistic education that integrates academic, physical, and spiritual development. Schools in countries like Japan and South Korea often incorporate mindfulness practices, such as meditation and yoga, into their daily routines. These practices help students develop focus, discipline, and emotional regulation.

In Scandinavian countries, the emphasis is on play-based learning and outdoor education. Countries like Finland and Denmark have implemented educational systems that prioritize creativity, collaboration, and experiential learning. Students spend a significant amount of time engaged in outdoor activities and project-based learning, which fosters a sense of curiosity and connection with nature.

In the United States and Canada, there is a growing interest in gamified learning and the use of technology to enhance education. Many schools are experimenting with educational apps, virtual reality experiences, and interactive games to make learning more engaging and accessible. Additionally, there is a focus on social-emotional learning and the integration of ethical discussions into the curriculum.

By exploring global perspectives on Edu-Play-tion, we can gain valuable insights into the diverse approaches to education and learn from each other's experiences. This cross-cultural exchange can help us create a more inclusive and innovative educational system that meets the needs of students around the world.

Book Description:

"Edu-Play-tion: How Gaming and Spirituality Are Revolutionizing Education" is an insightful exploration into the dynamic world of modern education. This book delves into the innovative ways gaming and spirituality are being integrated into the educational landscape to create a more engaging, inclusive, and holistic learning experience for students.

From the ancient methods of storytelling to the cutting-edge use of technology, education has always been a field of constant evolution. Now, as we embrace the intersection of play and learning, we are discovering the immense potential of gamified education. Through interactive games, virtual reality experiences, and educational apps, students are finding new ways to connect with their studies and enhance their understanding.

But education is not just about academics; it's also about personal growth and development. This book highlights the importance of incorporating spirituality into the curriculum, helping students develop emotional intelligence, resilience, and a sense of purpose. Mindfulness practices, ethical discussions, and community service projects are just a few of the ways spirituality is being woven into the fabric of education.

With chapters on the science of mindfulness, the benefits of ethical discussions, and the power of storytelling, "Edu-Play-tion" offers a comprehensive look at the future of education. The book also addresses the challenges and considerations of implementing these innovative approaches, providing practical strategies for educators and policymakers.

By exploring global perspectives and highlighting real-world examples, this book envisions a future where education is not only about imparting

CHAPTER 15: GLOBAL PERSPECTIVES ON EDU-PLAY-TION

knowledge but also about nurturing the mind, body, and spirit. "Edu-Play-tion: How Gaming and Spirituality Are Revolutionizing Education" is a must-read for anyone interested in the transformative power of education.

www.ingramcontent.com/pod-product-compliance
Lightning Source LLC
LaVergne TN
LVHW020501080526
838202LV00057B/6097